Freedom

An Amnesty International Glasgow Groups Exhibition

For Ma Thida (Myanmar), Hwang Suk-yong (South Korea)
and Manuel Manríquez San Agustín (Mexico),
prisoners of conscience.

Amnesty International

Amnesty International is a worldwide human rights movement. It has over a million members in 170 countries and territories. They all work to stop some of the gravest violations by governments of people's fundamental human rights. Amnesty International is impartial. It is independent of any government, political persuasion or religious creed.

Amnesty International campaigns to free all men, women and children detained anywhere for their beliefs, their ethnic origin, sex, colour or language - provided they have not used or advocated violence. These people are termed prisoners of conscience.

Amnesty International works for fair and prompt trials for political prisoners and works on their behalf when they are held without charge or trial. It opposes the death penalty, extrajudicial executions, "disappearances", torture and other cruel treatment of all prisoners.

Amnesty International also opposes abuses by opposition groups, including hostage-taking, torture and killing of prisoners.

Amnesty International works to promote all the human rights enshrined in the Universal Declaration of Human Rights, an international treaty drawn up in 1948, in the aftermath of the Second World War.

"Everyone has the right to freedom of thought, conscience and religion."

"All human beings are born free and equal in dignity and rights."

"No one shall be subjected to torture or to cruel, inhuman or degrading treatment or punishment."

"Everyone has the right to freedom of opinion and expression."

"Everyone has the right to life, liberty and security of person."

"Everyone has the right freely to participate in the cultural life of the community... [and] to enjoy the arts."

A selection from Articles from The Universal Declaration of Human Rights (United Nations General Assembly, 10 December, 1948).

Freedom

An Amnesty International Glasgow Groups Exhibition

presented in association with Ormeau Baths Gallery, Belfast

painting | sculpture | photography | video

Oladele Bamgboye

Mikey Cuddihy

Willie Doherty

Micky Donnelly

Brian Jenkins

Michael Mazière

Keith Piper

Jo Spence and Terry Dennett

Pavel Büchler

Avtarjeet Dhanjal

Rory Donaldson

Mona Hatoum

Tracy Mackenna

John Newling

Amanda Thesiger

Curator: Angela Kingston

Art Gallery & Museum, Kelvingrove, Glasgow,

29 September 1995 - 21 January 1996

Ormeau Baths Gallery, Belfast,

8 February - 15 March 1996

Southampton Art Gallery,

5 April - 2 June 1996

McManus Galleries, Dundee,

30 November 1996 - 27 January 1997

Contents

A history of the **Freedom** exhibition: part one

The story of the **Freedom** exhibition begins in 1990, when Glasgow became the European City of Culture. Amnesty International chose to mark this in a special way: on Burns Night, January 25th, a campaign was launched to free three artists who were prisoners of conscience - poets Jack Mapanje (Malawi) and Nguyen Chi Thien (Vietnam), and visual artist, Hong Song Dam (South Korea). One of the highlights of the campaign was a powerful exhibition of work by Hong Song Dam - a series of woodcuts showing dramatic scenes of violence and suffering in his home country. Many people who saw these images were moved by them, and added their voices to those calling for Hong Song Dam and the two writers to be set free. Throughout the year, children sent paintings and drawings to the prisoners, thousands of people wrote letters, and tens of thousands signed petitions asking for their release.

The campaign achieved all that we had hoped for. First Jack Mapanje was set free, then Nguyen Chi Thien, and finally the news reached us that Hong Song Dam had been released from prison. The success of the 1990 campaign was the inspiration for the **Freedom** exhibition. The concerns we had then are still as pressing today: artists are still being arrested and imprisoned, governments still seek to stifle freedom of expression and crush dissent.

In initiating an exhibition of art on the theme of freedom, our intention is to celebrate freedom of expression and to remember those to whom freedom is denied. This publication and the exhibition it accompanies are dedicated to three individual artists who are currently prisoners of conscience: Ma Thida, a writer and doctor from Myanmar (formerly Burma) who is serving a twenty-year sentence for campaigning for democracy; Hwang Suk-yong, a well-known novelist from South Korea, who annoyed his government by making a trip to North Korea and is now serving a seven year sentence; and Manuel Manríquez San Agustín, a musician and member of the Otomí indigenous community in Mexico, who was sentenced to twenty-four years on a murder charge based only on a "signed confession" extracted under torture.

During the exhibition and its tour, Amnesty International will be campaigning for the release of these prisoners of conscience.
Please help us fight for their freedom.

Ann Drummond and Hazel Mills
For the Amnesty International Glasgow Groups Exhibition Committee

2 A history of the **Freedom** exhibition: part two

As many contributors to this publication point out, the concept of "freedom" is almost overwhelming. It is so wide ranging and so significant a subject, it is almost impossible to know how to begin to address it. It may help to have a definition of the word, but any attempt to encapsulate its meaning soon seems highly perverse. Even a grasp on the scope of the word is elusive. "Freedom" can refer to fundamental, solemn principles, yet it can also refer to levity and spontaneity. It is used to describe universal values, yet it is also used in the context of highly personal, subjective experience. Projecting both our needs as individuals and our aspirations as a society - drives which are far from compatible at times - "freedom" is one of the most ambitious words we have.

Art and freedom have a close relationship. Freedom is found at the core of the impulse to make art. Freedom exists at the moment when art stirs in the mind of the viewer. Like freedom, art lays claim to an expansive territory, at times addressing the quirkiest individual impulse, and at other times, the broadest social imperative. Art feeds freedom, breaching mental boundaries, issuing challenges to society, quickening the pulse.

An exhibition of art for Amnesty International - a worldwide organisation of individuals fighting for freedom from oppression - on the subject of freedom is a project which registered immediately. As selector I decided to focus on two strands of recent art practice, which are not usually seen together in the same exhibition, and which I feel most closely engage with the concept. **Freedom** presents, on the one hand, work by artists who are motivated by a belief in the capacity of art to bring about change. Often emerging from the so-called margins of society, these artists grapple with issues of race, gender, sexuality, disability and class. Through their art, which they regard as a form of social activism, they participate in the struggle for representation of marginalised social groups. In this exhibition, their art draws attention to the freedoms which are at stake in the United Kingdom today. **Freedom**, on the other hand, juxtaposes this approach with art which makes a bid towards freedom through the language of art. For within abstract art there is a constant testing, a constant impulse to experiment, as a means to explore subconscious feelings and memories and as a means to find new spaces for new ways of thinking.

continued /

A central premise of the exhibition is that within art there is a rich exchange of energies between the political and the aesthetic - between the two "freedoms".

The process which led to the selection of the fifteen artists for the exhibition was necessarily fluid, open, buoyant and free. I visited a large number of artists, seeking out art which asserted itself as indispensable to the exhibition. I tried to allow the experience of looking at art to extend the limitations one inevitably has as an individual. I listened out for an all-important sense of recognition from artists with regard to the relationship of their art to freedom and I needed, not least, a firm interest from them in Amnesty International as an organisation. In many respects, the fifteen artists eventually chosen for the **Freedom** exhibition selected themselves. And in many cases, it was one or two particular pieces by an artist, perhaps made several years ago, which jumped out from the rest and demanded inclusion.

There is an obvious question, though, which needs to be asked: why include only artists based in the U.K. when Amnesty is an international organisation and when, moreover, its rules of impartiality largely prohibit campaigns which address the state of affairs in members' own countries? The answer is, in part, that it would be impossible for anyone at a single point on the globe to put together a representative sample of art relating to freedoms (and oppressions) throughout the world. The main reason, however, is that the exhibition is intended specifically for audiences in the U.K. **Freedom** seeks to engage people with many of the fundamental principles Amnesty International upholds, through art which has been made in the context in which we live and which touches upon aspects of our own experience. Freedom, after all, is a process in which each of us necessarily plays a part.

Angela Kingston, Curator
Born 1959 in Woking, lives in Birmingham

OLADELE AJIBOYE BAMGBOYE
BIRD OF PARADISE:
A PROFILE OF SEVEN YEARS
OF DESIRE 1989
photographic triptych
each part 127 x 102 cms

Oladele Ajiboye Bamgboye

Born 1963 in Odo-Eku, Nigeria; lives in London

I am concerned with: questions of sexuality with respect to an art practice informed by psychoanalysis; questions of cultural/personal identity; investigating and coming to terms with Yoruba (Nigerian) aesthetics within the Black Diaspora (the dispersed cultures of black peoples).

*In the photographs in **Freedom** elements are drawn from personal experience as a means to investigate the (black male) body as a site of conflict/crisis in meaning. Issues relating to sexual politics within postcolonialist art practice/cultural critique are fundamental to this work.*

I assert the freedom to attempt the deconstruction of Black Myths, to correct the voyeuristic perspective, and to attack prejudices which are constructed and maintained by fears of Black sexuality. I often employ the genre of self-portraiture: recognising that my work is challenging and risky, my presence signals that I am ultimately responsible for the statements I make.

PAVEL BÜCHLER

NO EASY ANSWERS (1995)

active feedback system

(a collaboration with Jim Lambert)

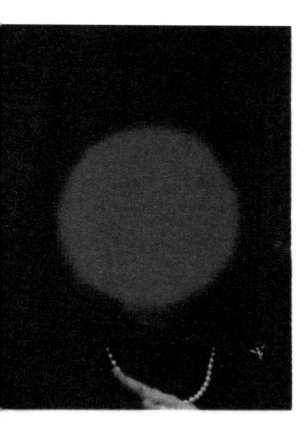

Pavel Büchler

Born 1952 in Prague, Czechoslovakia; lives in Glasgow

NEWSFLASH

I WAS READING ABOUT SOMEONE IN A NEWSPAPER. WHEN I FINISHED, I REALISED THAT THE ARTICLE WAS ABOUT ME. I TURNED TO ANOTHER STORY AND THAT TOO, ON REFLECTION, SEEMED TO BE ABOUT ME. I BEGAN READING A THIRD ONE AND SOON IT BECAME CLEAR THAT EVERYTHING IN THE PAPER WAS ABOUT ME. IT WAS ALL LIES.

I WAS WATCHING TELEVISION AND SAW SOMEONE ON THE NEWS. I DIDN'T RECOGNISE THE FACE BUT IT COULD HAVE BEEN MINE, EXCEPT FOR THE NOSE, THE CHIN, THE LIPS AND, OF COURSE, THE EYES. IT WAS A FACE WITHOUT A NAME.

I WAS LISTENING TO THE RADIO AND HEARD MY VOICE ASKING QUESTIONS (THAT I DIDN'T UNDERSTAND) AND MY VOICE ANSWERING. BUT THERE WERE NO ANSWERS.

I LOOKED IN THE MIRROR AND SAW MYSELF WHISPERING INTO SOMEONE'S EAR. MY VOICE VANISHED LIKE A DREAM. I THOUGHT: "JUST AS VISION IS DAZZLED BY LIGHT, SO SPEECH DROWNS IN WORDS".

MIKEY CUDDIHY

IN CARAGLOOS (1990)

acrylic and gesso on canvas

244 x 183 cms

Mikey Cuddihy

Born 1952 in New York, U.S.A.; lives in London

By using doodles and a kind of automatism as a source for my paintings, I'm trying to tap into a 'free' self; I'm interested in an unselfconscious order that comes into place eventually.

I need the freedom to be able to re-invent painting for myself, to question current orthodoxies: that decoration and the feminine are weak, for example; that lightness is synonymous with superficiality.

I never take painting for granted: when I'm planning new work, I often go through various completely different ways and means and forms it could take. So it's actually a surprise to find myself making a painting at the conclusion of that process.

WILLIE DOHERTY
FACTORY (IN A CORNER)
(1995)
diptych
2 cibachrome prints on aluminium
122 x 183 cms

Willie Doherty

Born 1959 in Derry, N. Ireland, where he continues to live

Willie Doherty's simple yet compelling large-scale photographs depict the rural and urban landscape in and around Derry.
A recent series of photographs was taken of the devastated interior of a factory. Despite their subject matter, these photographs
have a strangely ordinary quality. Yet their sumptuous detail and fastidious composition suggest a worrying over-familiarity
with violence. Combined with these impressions is an almost overwhelming sense of being unable to connect with the reality
of violence. Doherty's work gives rise to an uneasy exploration of issues of conflict and identity. (A.K.)

Rory Donaldson

Born 1965 in Edinburgh, lives in Glasgow

The content of my work reflects a personal interpretation of my surroundings and therefore I work with many different themes and differing modes of presentation. My work in the **Freedom** *exhibition focuses to a large extent on male identity. I have looked at issues that affect gay men, such as the age of consent debate, HIV and AIDS, 'pretend families', and the notion of victimless crime where two male adults can still be arrested for having consensual sex.*

Art is at its most powerful when it combines both aesthetics and content, each informing the other. I do not believe that art can change the world but it can question some of society's perceived realities.

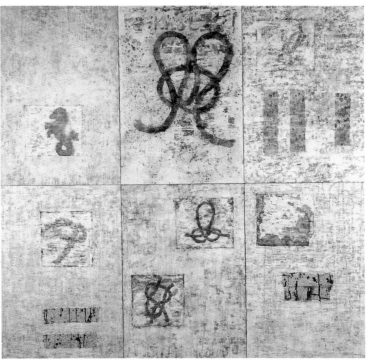

Micky Donnelly

Born in Belfast in 1952, lives in Belfast

The fabric of my work (paintings, drawings, installations) is informed by the extraordinary events in Ireland in recent times and the perceived need to respond in an innovative manner. Behind the references to objects and images associated with certain events, there lies a desire to challenge accepted forms of cultural identity and a sympathy for a certain kind of political change. These impulses constitute a type of freedom of intention which probably has little to do with how the work is actually read. It has been said that the recent work has a dominant mood of fragility or a sense of loss, recalled or imminent. That's also intended and maybe that's all that matters. In an exhibition, the work takes on a certain momentum and the original impulses are subsumed by other forces and by the more contingent freedoms of interpretation.

Brian Jenkins

Born 1964 in Falkirk, lives in Falkirk and Luxembourg

For some time I wondered what I could write about 'freedom'. It is, for sure, a loaded subject meaning many things to many people. Since last year I have worked with a group of residents from the Hôpital Neuro-Psychiatrique in Ettelbruck, Luxembourg. There I continuously question and grapple with the notion of freedom, as do the people I work with. Some have lived in the hospital for as long as thirty or forty years, more or less behind lock and key. I asked Jos, one of the people I work with, what freedom meant to him:

"I have been here, off and on, for thirty years now. I arrived on 4th July 1965 for two and a half months of observation. Then I spent the next ten years with my parents before becoming ill again. I was hospitalised for ten months. My father died. Over the following years, while staying with my mother, I would attend the hospital on an irregular basis, staying maybe several weeks at a time. My mother went into an old people's home in Useldange; she died some time later. I visited her as much as I could. Nine years ago I came into hospital. I've been here ever since.

Freedom is relative - it is how one imagines it. You can never put freedom and thoughts into prison."

Jos Kolbusch, 21 July 1995 (translation, used with permission)

BRIAN JENKINS
THE MULTIPLICATION
OF BREAD AND FISH
(1995)
polaroid photographs
each 11 x 9 cms

Tracy Mackenna

Born 1963 in Scotland, lives in Glasgow

In **Flash Couplets**, *successive pairs of words emerge from the distance, dissolving as they are replaced by new words. Hypnotic movement and intense colour conceal at first the opposing nature of the paired words (such as* flatter *and* wound). *In the silence a rhythm builds. Accumulatively, the words start to suggest the emotional territory of an intimate relationship. The riskiness and fragility of the situation gradually become apparent and it finally emerges that misunderstandings are acute and potentially dangerous. In this imagined dialogue, a perhaps unwitting aggressor impinges on the freedom of another, possibly less powerful person.*

In all my work, I seek to expose the frailties inherent in almost every human exchange. Within this act of exposure is a desire for change.

Michael Mazière

Born in Grenoble, France, in 1957; lives in London

As a child I always wondered why films were not made from the viewpoint of the main character, and I already had a desire for an expression free of the limits of language. My films and videos attempt to reach a condition close to a 'dream state' – a place outside of the restrictions that the telling of a story imposes, connected to the realm of the unconscious.

The state of being free from boundaries and rules is an unknown and difficult territory that art, the impossible project, should strive to touch.

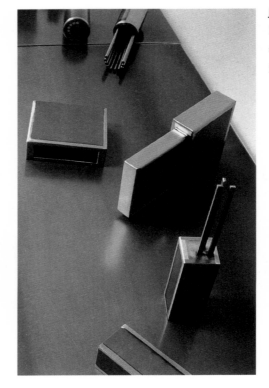

JOHN NEWLING
EXITS (1988)
multiple part steel sculpture
563 x 106 x 46 cms

John Newling

Born 1952 in Birmingham, lives in Nottingham

Do you remember your first bicycle?

When you rode it without support did you feel lighter?

Have you ever spun on the spot to make yourself dizzy?

Did you enjoy the fall?

Why is Heaven up and Hell down?

Why are bells and birds such popular motifs for freedom?

If choice is a freedom then why is shopping so stressful?

Do you remember your first kiss?

Did it make you slightly giddy?

Do you remember the times when you made a complete idiot of yourself and others forgave you?

Do these moments of forgiveness help you to sleep?

Why do circuses need flying trapeze acts?

Have you ever won on the instant lottery?

Was it thrilling?

Did it make you light-headed?

Have you ever been on a fairground ride that filled you with dread?

Did you feel a sense of achievement?

Did it make your head spin?

Why do angels need wings?

Why do we need angels to need wings?

KEITH PIPER
stills from
TAGGING THE OTHER
(1991)
*four Amiga-generated
computer animations plus
projected image*

Keith Piper

Born in Malta in 1960; lives in London

"Pan-European ethnicity was forged, initially, in violent opposition to non-whites. Mongols, Turks, Moors... and later in opposition to Africans, Asians and New World Indigenes (with Jews providing a handy Internal Eastern Question)."
Scott L. Malcomson, **Heart of Whiteness***.*

During the traumatic progress of the nations of Western Europe towards greater economic and social union, anxieties around what constitutes a 'European citizen' have come to the fore. The proposed lowering of internal borders has in turn led to demands for the strengthening of external controls against a feared influx of 'non-European' migrants from Africa and Asia in a scenario which has been dubbed 'Fortress Europe'. These anxieties have in turn spawned an escalation in the use of technologies of surveillance and control to monitor not only the movements of non-white peoples across borders, but also to 'tag' and scrutinise the occupants of non-white communities across the European continent.

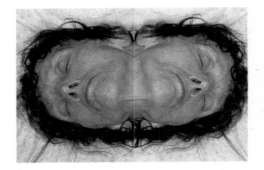 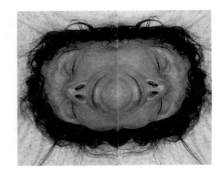

Jo Spence and Terry Dennett

Jo Spence was born in London in 1934; she died in London in 1992
Terry Dennett was born in 1938 in London, where he continues to live

Metamorphosis *was pre-planned and scripted shortly before Jo Spence's death. It was conceived at a time when the leukaemia which eventually killed her had already made it difficult for her to sustain the energy to take her own pictures – and when she was finally forced to think seriously about the possibility of dying.*

The concepts behind **Metamorphosis** *are diverse. Most importantly, it underlines her desire as a socialist feminist to continue to deal with taboo subjects in such a way that the boundaries of what is thought permissible as images of women would be extended just that little bit more. Death and sex, she observed, were still two of the biggest hang-ups in our society.*
Terry Dennett

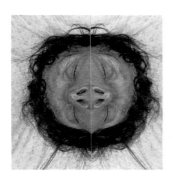 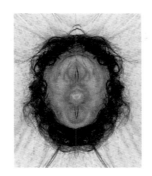

METAMORPHOSIS
(1991-2)
Do we have the right to
determine our own images
of ourselves after death?
A pre - and post - death
collaboration
framed photographs

24

Amanda Thesiger

Born in Surrey, 1964; lives in London

The images in my paintings evolve intuitively. Forays into the unconscious and processes of free association allow me to depart from the ordinary and familiar, and the near chaos which results is liberating.

Breaking free from obvious outside references, the paintings become 'outlandish' or 'otherworldly'. My works seek out those fleeting moments of reverie which transcend reality.

MONA HATOUM
stills from
SO MUCH I WANT TO SAY
(1983)
5 minute black & white video
A Western Front Video Production,
Vancouver, Canada

Mona Hatoum

Palestinian, born in Beirut, Lebanon, 1952; lives in London

*When Mona Hatoum was 23, she came to England on a visit and stayed on when the outbreak of civil war in Lebanon prevented her returning. While the conflict was raging during the seventies and eighties, she feared for her family's safety and rarely saw them. For long periods it was impossible to phone them, or even to be sure they would receive her letters. Meanwhile she was living in London, effectively an exile. Her video, **So much I want to say**, was made during this time.*

A series of still images unfolds (one every eight seconds), revealing the face of a woman (the artist) filling the screen. Two male hands repeatedly gag the woman and obscure parts of her face, sometimes covering it completely. On the sound-track, repeated over and over again, are the words "so much I want to say" spoken by a female (the artist's) voice. (A.K.)

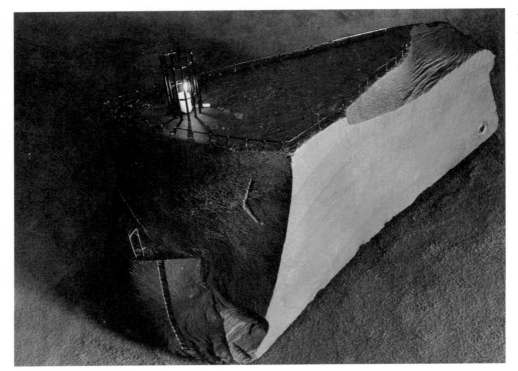

AVTARJEET DHANJAL
A CANDLE (1995)
slate, metal, candle
101 x 51 x 58 cms

26

Avtarjeet Dhanjal

Born 1939 in Dalla, Punjab; lives in Shropshire

A seed has its own in-built energy to grow and blossom. But for a meticulous gardener even a flower can become inconvenient. Social gardeners like flowers to follow and comply with existing rules, and inconvenient flowers are either eliminated or moved away from the well trimmed lawns of society. Some of these flowers still blossom, leaving a fragrance on our path for generations to come.

    Their contribution can be compared with that of a candle burning to brighten our path. It can easily be ignored or blown out, yet it has the capacity to light another thousand candles.

    *I believe an artist's role is to be an observer and possibly a commentator. He or she may also play another important role as a catalyst. My sculpture **A Candle** is an observation.*

We gave Guy Brett the task of writing about the relationship of art and freedom. He quickly found that this subject was not going to yield to description when approached directly. In his experience, what matters most here vanishes at the moment it is named. His solution is a circuitous route via definitions of wit and irony which give way to a series of stirring proposals.

AROUND THE SUBJECT
by Guy Brett

If there are two kinds of everything, there are two kinds of laughter. One is cold and hideous, contemptuous and cruel. The other is warm, obviously. But this opposite kind of laughter, which I want to write about, is so ordinary, so prevalent, that it could almost be called the normal state of life, the lubricant of life as against gloom, inertia and death.

It could also be called a form of bravado, of course, a protection against fear. But why not? Fear is also everyday and continuous, constant company, and then sudden and overwhelming. Laughter is found at both moments. I remember a phrase I read in an old book I picked up in a secondhand bookshop. It was the 'autobiography' of an Australian aboriginal, in which the author, through a ghost writer, spoke of the atmosphere of the community. A phrase always lodged in my mind: *"Ripples of mirth are constantly rolling from our camps ... "* [1]

These words immediately reminded me of the quality that Mikhail Bakhtin, in his writings on Rabelais, has described as the essence of Rabelaisian Pantagruelism: the ability *"to be cheerful, wise and kind"* .[2] Pantagruelism was identified with the feast, itself derived from the Platonic symposium, a form of sociability which was also a genre of literature. At the Pantagruelian feast, *"conversations get going, conversations which are wise but filled as well with laughter and banter"*.[3] There was a general lack of all forms of up-tightness, closer to a love-feast than to today's academic 'debates'.

Such everyday images may be followed by one of the human being *in extremis*:

> I felt as if a gigantic serpent bored the earth, until it became so unhinged it could never be returned. I felt, since the mercy of the moment prevented me from seeing, that I was compelled to remain inside a barbarous demolition. I felt, as after every earthquake in which I have been, the instinctive need to get hold of a living being, which is the other way to become aware of your absolute loneliness. I also felt a sort of emotional catatonia, the fierce sensation that madness is right there, side by side with death, until a joke heard amidst the shadows reveals to yourself, by the laugh, that you are alive. [4]

These were the words of a woman earthquake survivor in Cauquenes, a small town in the south of Chile, as reported by the national newspaper *El Mercurio*. The words of Waipuldanya, the Australian aboriginal, were ghost-written by a certain Douglas Lockwood, a correspondent for the *Melbourne Herald* group of newspapers. The way in which both these statements 'ring true', in their very wording, is itself a testimony to the survival of 'life experience' through layers of official, ideologically-influenced mediation.

The modern definition of wit as *"amusing verbal cleverness"* has taken the place of a much broader meaning. In the Renaissance, wit was associated with *"intellectual keenness and a capacity of 'invention' by which writers could discover ... resemblances between apparently dissimilar things".*[5] The French word for wit is the same as for spirit, *esprit*; it is possible to link intelligence, imagination, humour, wisdom and spirituality in a single concept.[6] In fact the techniques of the different approaches to wisdom can often be surprisingly similar. Oscar Wilde's witty aphorisms were almost always based on a paradoxical reversal of the received, stereotypical, 'straight' wisdom. For example:

> *Anybody can act. Most people in England do nothing else. To be conventional is to be a comedian.*[7]

Similarly, spiritual techniques such as those of Zen are also based on paradox, beginning with the paradoxical problem that one obscures reality by naming it. As the poet dom Sylvester Houedard put it:

> *Everything material is a revelation of the unseen - the ultimate truth about truth is painted on everything material for all who can read - i.e. god is known only as not this (neti), i.e. not thing (nada) or nothing.*[8]

Here a word has been used to convey the idea of no-word. This alerts us to the fact that the 'affirmative negation' can also be a look, a gesture, the handling of material, or other bodily action.

Irony itself has been defined as a contradictory and bi-directional device. According to D.C. Muecke, irony has a gyroscopic function of *"keeping life liveable"*; it can be used both to destabilise the excessively stable and established, and to stabilise the unstable, arbitrary and chaotic.[9] No wonder that irony is on so many people's lips today with our essentially contradictory and ambivalent feelings about almost all phenomena. Reality must seem full of ironies when so many 'good ideas' seem to turn inexorably into 'bad things', and so many once-emancipatory notions become new sources of oppression.

It seems to be the institutionalisation and bureaucratisation of good ideas which turns them bad. This may simply be a process by which long-running patterns of power and privilege continue to run. The institutionalisation produces an 'anti-' (as in anti-art, but the process takes place in every field of culture). Anti-art is (or was) anti the institution of art in the name of reviving art's connection with life. There are many definitions of this more open and experimental field in which art may operate. Here is one by an artist:

> I believe that art can function as a critique of existing culture, and as a locus where futures not otherwise possible can begin to shape themselves.[10]

However, the future that art intimates must have something transcendent about it if it has been intimated by art. Art has a transformational character; it transcends sheer beauty and ugliness, sheer pleasure and pain. Art cannot be a social blueprint. It appeals to something inside, and perhaps its recognition comes from the same source, and has the same quality of quickening life, as the laugh.

1   *I, The Aboriginal*, by Douglas Lockwood, Adelaide: Rigby Ltd, 1962, p145

2   *The Dialogic Imagination*, by Mikhail Bakhtin (edited by Michael Holquist, translated by Caryl Emerson and Michael Holquist), Austin: University of Texas Press, 1981, p186

3   Ibid, p187

4   Quoted in *Nine Survivors*, an Airmail Painting by Eugenio Dittborn (1986), from a report in *El Mercurio* of March 1985.

5   *The Concise Oxford Dictionary of Literary Terms*, by Chris Baldick, Oxford: Oxford University Press, 1990

6   And more besides. "Esprit, n.m. Spirit, ghost; soul, vital breath, vital principle; mind, sense, understanding, intellect; wit; fancy; humour, disposition, temper, character, meaning; spirits, spiritous liquor; breathing, aspirate." *Cassell's New French Dictionary*, 1962.

7   Quoted in Richard Ellmann, *Oscar Wilde*, Penguin Books, 1988, p 349

8   *The Cosmic Typewriter*, by dom Sylvester Houedard

9   *Irony and the Ironic*, by D.C. Muecke, London: Methuen, 1982, p 4

10 Susan Hiller, interviewed in *Fuse*, Toronto, November/December 1981

Guy Brett

Guy Brett is a writer and critic. He was born in 1942 in Yorkshire, and lives in London.